I0224495

"When you conquer what is within you, no opponent can. This book dives into what it takes to take over you so you can take over the competition."
— Geo Derice

ART OF THE FIGHT

MENTAL PERFORMANCE FOR MARTIAL ARTISTS

ART OF THE FIGHT

MENTAL PERFORMANCE FOR MARTIAL ARTISTS

SEPANO HASSANZADEH

Copyright © 2026 by Sepano Hassanzadeh

Cover Design: Tri W.
Interior Design: Christopher Derrick for Unauthorized Media

All rights reserved. No part of this publication may be reproduced, used, performed, stored in a retrieval system, or transmitted in any form or by any means, electronic, mechanical, photocopying, recording, or otherwise, without the prior written permission of the author, except for brief quotations in critical articles or reviews.

The author of this book does not dispense health or medical advice. This book offers information of a general nature to support your pursuit of maximum success and performance. It is not designed to be a definitive guide or to replace advice from a qualified professional. There is no guarantee that the methods suggested in this book will be successful, and any training carries risk. Thus, neither the publisher nor the author assumes liability for any losses that may be sustained by the use of the methods described in this book, and any such liability is expressly disclaimed. If you use any of the information in this book, you assume full responsibility for your actions.

First edition, June 2020
Revised edition, March 2026
ISBN-13: 978-1-7365941-0-0

Printed in the United States of America

This book is dedicated to every person I've ever had the honor and privilege of coaching, helping, and inspiring. Each of you has uniquely helped pave my way on this continuous and fulfilling path as a teacher.

I also dedicate this book to anyone battling mental health challenges. If you are struggling, please keep fighting. It may not seem like it now, but better days do lie ahead, and peace can be found. Sometimes you must press on just a little longer, keeping your healing in sight. A pause is not a fall, so never give up. To those who have conquered their mental demons, be a beacon of light for others. Know that your greatest struggles can lend you power and compassion beyond measure.

CONTENTS

INTRODUCTION

What does a normal 14-year-old boy do with his time? Go to high school? Play video games? Hang out with friends? How about studying the powers of the mind, researching the hidden capabilities of the subconscious, and learning how to reprogram reality through self-talk and suggestion? That's the kind of kid I was, and it gives you an idea of why this book you're holding (or viewing) came to be. My interest in the mind and its connection to performance started early.

Battles with mental health brought the mind to the forefront of my priorities. Navigating middle and high school with epilepsy was just episode one. Then came serious physical illnesses during college, including pneumonia and other major setbacks. Finally, I faced psychological struggles that sidelined me heavily. Any one of these could have easily derailed someone on their path to becoming their best.

Yet a burning desire to better myself, to become the strongest version of myself, kept me going. That passion for the mind's power became a vital foundation, anchoring me despite the obstacles I faced. As I overcame these challenges, at least by my own estimation, a deep longing grew to help others on their journeys as well.

LEARNED THROUGH MARTIAL ARTS

In my early years, I didn't fully grasp how powerful the mental component really was. While playing competitive tennis in high school and college, my mental game was admittedly weak. My performance in practice was great, but in competition it fell short. That didn't change until I picked up combat sports.

As I started training in martial arts, my inner flame burned hotter and brighter. That's where my deep passion was truly awakened. Through studying and practicing various fighting disciplines, I began to discover myself. My mental game sharpened, and my desire to fully understand the mind's power emerged.

I earned my bachelor's degree in psychology, and later a master's in sports psychology. Alongside this path, I worked as a personal trainer, self-defense instructor, and wellness coach. My experience in martial arts set the foundation for my life and directly impacts my well-being today. These experiences shaped me into the person I am: a stronger, more confident man, and a coach whose principles and philosophy are rooted in essential martial arts wisdom. Those values have driven me to contribute through coaching and to write this book, with the hope that others will pursue greatness through the lessons martial arts has given me.

MY BACKGROUND

Before we go further, in the interest of full transparency, let me offer a disclaimer: I am not a professional fighter, nor have I competed in professional bouts. Don't let that discount the lessons I share here. I've had significant in-ring and sparring experience and understand what takes place under stressful, combative conditions. Over the years, I've trained in Muay Thai, Brazilian Jiu-Jitsu, boxing, and various other arts. I've been in the same high-stress situations fighters face. I know the physical demands of training and what it takes to perform at a high level. I know what is required of a combat athlete, physically and, more importantly, mentally.

I've spent a decade in fitness and performance coaching, helping athletes improve both physically and mentally. While my own fighting history isn't extensive, there's a story I would be remiss not to share: my last fight in 2017.

Leading up to that amateur bout, my mental state was challenged and dampened by many factors. Looking back, if I hadn't cultivated my mind and drawn strength from knowing and being myself, I'm not sure I'd be able to speak of the triumph I experienced that day, despite the unexpected disadvantage I faced.

I CAN'T QUIT

Within the first 12 seconds of that fight, my opponent landed a clean head kick that sent me to the canvas. I broke my fall with my elbow and forearm and sprang back up from what was counted as a flash knockdown. But something was wrong: my left shoulder was clearly and visibly dislocated. Panic, defeat, and humiliation flooded my mind. The crowd, including friends, loved ones, and teammates, had just watched me get knocked down before the fight had even begun. Now my shoulder was wrecked, and my entire game plan, along with my left arm, was gone. What was I going to do?

It was a severe disadvantage. Anyone would think I was doomed. But quitting wasn't a decision my mind could accept. This is where all the mental conditioning and martial arts training came through. I kept pushing, blocking out pain, digging deep, and tapping into the person who had trained so rigorously for this moment. Instead of being consumed by the nightmare, I used the adrenaline-fueled survival state to tap into the power of my mind. "Flight" was never an option. I began to outwork my opponent, applying nonstop offensive pressure with my right hand and knees in the clinch. Eventually, I won the bout via TKO, as my opponent could not continue. That victory was not about technical or physical performance. It was a demonstration of the mental game, the inner game.

It is in these testing moments that we truly learn about ourselves. While I'm not a clinical psychologist or a professional athlete, I am a student and warrior of this game called life. My combined studies and personal trials position me to share a framework that can help you find triumph, in the ring and in life.

WHAT IS THIS BOOK ABOUT?

This book is about mental performance training for martial artists and combat athletes. That means learning about your mind, the mental processes within it, and developing awareness of your inner world so you can guide your body and mind to perform at your best. When an athlete strengthens this connection, performance improves.

Any personal blockages, whether related to confidence, purpose, fear, or anxiety, are what this book is designed to address. The goal is to sharpen your mental skills so you can overcome internal barriers.

WHY MENTAL SKILLS TRAINING FOR MARTIAL ARTISTS SPECIFICALLY

Mental skills have become a greater focus for high performers over the past two decades. Top athletes endorse meditation apps and work with peak performance coaches. But how much is this talked about in the martial arts and fight community, and how does it differ?

Mental skills training involves the same basic processes in any sport or art. What's different for combat athletes is the unique demands of the sport. As Joe Rogan described on his podcast, fighting, especially MMA, is "high-level problem solving with very dire consequences if you fail." There's a sense of urgency and a tiny margin for error. In both striking and grappling arts, a single lapse in focus can be dangerous. Even with rules, the consequences of being mentally unprepared can be serious.

This is what sets the psychology of combat sports apart. Both the physical and mental demands are high and immediate, and failing to meet them can have serious consequences.

TWO KEY ELEMENTS: RELAXED AND ALERT

When it comes to the mental game for martial artists, there are two essential elements. I first heard about this from my Muay Thai coach, who learned it from the legendary Bas Rutten. He always emphasized the importance of being "relaxed and ready," which I'd reframe as relaxed and alert. We'll dive deeper into this concept in a later chapter, but here's a quick overview.

One side of the coin is achieving the proper level of relaxation. By "proper," I mean optimal. Too much relaxation and you become physically lax, dull, and sluggish in your actions and reactions. Under these conditions, mental lapses can easily occur, leading to the kinds of serious consequences we discussed earlier.

The flip side is proper alertness. Optimal alertness means having the right level of energy, arousal, or excitation at the right moments. Too much energy, however, can lead to nervousness, which burns out both body and mind. Physically, you deplete yourself and fatigue too early. Mentally, you become overly alert and fall into a narrow, tunnel-vision focus. In these states, you either miss vital opportunities to attack, defend, or counter, or you become too exhausted to perform effectively, again putting you in the territory of serious consequences.

This is where mental conditioning comes in: to help us achieve a balanced flow between relaxation and alertness. Through proper training, you can drastically minimize, and even eliminate, those errors, lapses, and negative outcomes that result from being either too relaxed or too alert.

THE MISSING LINK FOUND

What is the key to achieving what you want in performance, and ultimately in life? What is the secret to consistently crushing your goals and attaining whatever you desire? It begins and ends on the mental plane. When we look at athletes at the highest level and ask how they got there, one common denominator stands out, separating them from everyone else: mindset. Sure, there is talent, which many great athletes possess. But what distinguishes those at the very top? It is mastery of the inner game. By working with sport psychology professionals, these athletes have learned to maximize their physical talents by enhancing their mental skills and bringing out their true greatness.

Wouldn't you want to experience the same? Tapping into your true potential and bringing out your greatness no longer has to be a dream reserved for a select few. ART of the Fight is designed to reveal what I consider the missing link to maximizing physical talent and performance. This book fills a void in the martial arts world by providing a crucial framework that shows combat athletes, at any level, how to access a higher, stronger, and better version of themselves through mastery of natural performance enhancement, a kind of self-evolution, if you will.

If there was ever a "secret weapon" or "something more" that top athletes in combat sports seem to have, this would be the closest thing. It's the invisible force that resides within. It's knowing yourself inside and out, without a shred of doubt. It is, ultimately, understanding the ART of mental conditioning, which we will break down in the upcoming sections of this book.

SECTION ONE
AIMING

CHAPTER 1
ATTENTION

"The greatest scientists are artists as well."
— *Albert Einstein*

K nown by many as one of the smartest men to have ever lived, Albert Einstein once said that the greatest scientists are also artists. This idea is relevant here because, while there is a physical element, a science, to mastering martial arts, there is also a very real art. In this book, we merge science and art to help you uncover the greatness within. Combining these two worlds will help you reach your desired performance level and become unstoppable.

As stated at the end of the introduction, there is a system, a framework, that I've developed through my own studies and life experiences to help you master your mental training. Throughout the rest of this book, we will dive into each of the three parts that make up ART.

A.R.T. BREAKDOWN

As you might guess, ART is an acronym. The "A" stands for Aiming, the "R" for Resonating, and the "T" for Tuning. These are your pillars, the building blocks of a framework for enhancing yourself on a mental level.

Within each letter of the acronym are three sub-levels that build upon each other to form the complete picture. Each level leads to the next, creating a brick-by-brick approach to uncovering and building the optimal you. It's essential not to skip any of these levels, as they are designed to be followed in sequence. You cannot fully grasp a level without first having a complete understanding of the one before it.

It's also important to note that there isn't a set timeframe for advancing from level to level. Each individual is different, so the pace of progress will depend on your personal ability, understanding, and experience.

Here are the sub-levels for each stage, to give you a preview of the journey we're about to embark on. I'm excited to guide you down this path toward the ultimate destination: Triumph.

The Aiming stage begins with Attention. Next comes Awareness. Finally, in this section, we reach Action.

The Resonating stage starts with Realization, followed by Revelation, and concludes with Rise.

Finally, the Tuning stage starts with Technique, then progresses to Training, and concludes at the final destination, the ultimate summation of all the stages and phases in this book: Triumph. It's fitting that the conclusion is both an arrival and a departure of sorts, a new beginning and a transformed reality of performance.

ATTENTION DEFINED

This chapter has us diving into the first level of the Aiming stage: Attention. According to Webster's Dictionary, attention is defined as "the act or state of applying the mind to something." Before proceeding further, it's important to note that everything shared in this book is based on a combination of research and personal experience. I define attention as energy, or more specifically, as "mental currency." When you "pay attention," you are giving that mental energy or currency to whatever you're focusing on. Where you place your energy is where everything begins. To drive the point home, I'll share a simple quote: "Energy flows where attention goes."

The journey of self-enhancement begins here, at this first level. It starts with our energy. In theory, there is an infinite amount of energy we can tap into mentally. Our physical state, of course, plays a role in this, but that's a separate discussion. When we talk about attention, the first question to ask is, "What has it?" What is using up that precious mental currency? For many of us, that mental energy is dedicated to any number of issues or problems we're facing at any given moment in the day.

For the athlete or coach reading this book, this is the perfect opportunity to tap into the power of personal problem-solving, or "self-solving." When we are able to focus on the problem at hand, we create space for its solution, along with a roadmap for getting there. Attention is the metaphorical act of lacing up our shoes and preparing to tackle the obstacles and challenges ahead with a game plan.

ENERGY BLOCKERS

The idea that energy flows where attention goes is not new, yet why is it that so many people are unable to get what they want? What blocks people's ability to effectively manage their energy? In short, it's a lack of knowledge. That, combined with limiting belief systems, can prevent athletes from channeling the power of attention.

One common issue among athletes is the belief that the problem holding them back is rooted in the physical. This is the athlete who keeps pushing their body further and harder, convinced that something is physically lacking and that the only solution lies in working harder. While this effort is admirable, it's often like trying to fit a round peg into a square hole. It simply doesn't work. More force only creates more damage, and with more damage comes greater disappointment and frustration.

In situations like this, athletes must realize the tremendous power of their thoughts. Thoughts become things. I'll repeat that: our thoughts become things. By discounting the mind and focusing solely on the body, we hit a dead end. We can't truly tap into infinite energy, which can only be accessed through the mental realm.

Alongside the lack of knowledge holding athletes back are limiting belief systems. Using the same example, the athlete who puts in effort without getting the desired result starts mentally programming themselves to believe there's no solution. This idea solidifies into a limiting belief, and the athlete repeats it as their prevailing "mental script." This belief system dictates that improvement is difficult, immediately creating personal limitations. For this athlete, the journey ends long before triumph can ever be experienced.

Attention is being used in the scenarios above, but it isn't facilitative, meaning it does not help or serve the athlete at all. Instead, that mental currency is spent reinforcing the belief that change is difficult or impossible, that "this is just the way it's going to be." It becomes the athlete's most undesired self-fulfilling prophecy, devastating and self-defeating in nature.

You can begin to see just how vital this first step is. How you use attention, by choosing where to direct it, matters greatly. Instead of focusing on what you can't do, start giving that mental energy to what you can do. Doing so will shift your reality in a more desirable direction. It's merely a single thought away, so pay attention.

CHAPTER 2
AWARENESS

"What is necessary to change a person
is to change his awareness of himself."
— *Abraham Maslow*

n the last chapter, we learned about the usefulness of attention and how energy flows wherever our attention goes. With this foundation, the next level in the Aiming stage is Awareness. Now that we're paying attention properly, we can begin to orient ourselves on the path of self-enhancement. This is where we start putting intention into our attention. It's where we start asking questions like, "Where are we guiding this energy?"

The Awareness phase is all about putting our attention into action. That's the simplest way to describe it. Think of it like this: in the last chapter, you, the reader, became aware of the concept of attention. You now recognize that this energy exists and understand its importance. With this knowledge, the next questions are, "What am I to do with this?" and "How can I maximize this newfound knowledge to get me where I want to be?"

Here's an interesting way to look at how attention and awareness work together: attention, this mental energy, is your employee.

With awareness, you learn how to best employ that energy to do the work that produces desired results. This is a powerful concept. Go back and reread that. This analogy illustrates the utility of attention when it's implemented with awareness. Together, they set the foundation in the Aiming stage, enabling you to take the next step forward and upward.

THE MIRROR

Awareness is not just about where you are directing your attention; it also serves as a mirror, an opportunity for reflection. It gives us the ability to look back on how we have managed our attention and see where it has taken us. Too often, we neglect to reflect on what we've been doing and evaluate whether it has been moving us toward or away from our desired destination. This is why it's so important not to skip this step.

Self-awareness is one of the highest forms of knowledge one can possess. It's what allows an individual like Bruce Lee to realize that instead of learning 10,000 different kicks, it's more effective to practice one kick 10,000 times. This level of awareness, knowing exactly what you need in order to succeed, will lead you naturally to the final phase of the Aiming stage: Action.

By now, you can hopefully see that there are levels to this, and that there is an order to the "madness" that occurs in our heads. Once you understand this process, you can truly become unstoppable by tapping into the infinite potential within. This leads to the triumph of experiencing an ideal version of yourself, which few ever get to witness in their lifetime.

CHAPTER 3
ACTION

"Action is the foundational key to all success"
— Pablo Picasso

f you were on the set of a film or television series, this is what you would hear: until the word "action" is uttered, nothing moves and nothing happens. Pablo Picasso, the famous Spanish painter and sculptor, said that "action is the foundational key to all success." If you wish to triumph, having attention and awareness alone is not enough. Action is the final piece needed to overcome the obstacles and barriers standing in your way. With action, you make real movement toward self-discovery and its byproduct, performance enhancement. This "awakening" is exactly what must occur before we enter Section Two of this book: the Resonating stage.

The purpose of the Aiming stage is to gain clarity on the underlying elements that stand in our way. It's about identifying where focus is needed in order to begin the process of evolving and building toward one's best, most optimized self. When attention and awareness merge, they produce action. Knowing that you have an ocean of mental energy that you can employ and direct leads you to this final step: applying these forces to create positive change and transformation.

SUBOPTIMAL & WRONG ACTIONS

To help you better understand and master the Aiming stage, let me provide a real-world example that captures the workings of attention, awareness, and action. For this, we'll take a look at my past training, specifically how my lack of understanding of my own strengths limited my fighting ability.

When I look back at past performances, primarily in sparring, I realize how little I was using some of my greatest strengths. I have a long reach, along with a good, fast jab and a strong front kick (teep), yet I rarely used these as primary weapons to dictate the fight. I was too conservative, confining my fighting ability to a narrow range compared to what it could have been, and what it is now. I exerted a lot of energy and effort fighting in a certain way, one that was suboptimal for me, and I became rigid in a set style while remaining blind to my greater potential.

Instead of dedicating my energy with full confidence to honing my ideal fighting style, I misdirected it. As a result, I was nowhere near as effective as I am now, or as I could have been then. Of course, there's much more technical detail I could share about this example, but the point here is not to discuss fighting strategy. Rather, I want to illustrate how keen awareness of your strengths can be a major game-changer. When you know exactly what you're capable of, you can train with great confidence and focused purpose. Without this knowledge, you're likely making suboptimal choices at best and taking ineffective actions at worst. You may still improve, but ultimately, you're wasting potential and drastically limiting your abilities.

UNTAPPED STRENGTH

When I think of someone unable to access their true potential, a story that comes to mind is the tale of the circus elephant. This story illustrates how diminishing it can be to never recognize one's own untapped reservoir of potential. Although the original source of the tale is unknown, I'll paraphrase it here.

The story speaks of a baby elephant brought into the circus. Its leg is tied to a wooden stake driven into the ground. At first, the baby elephant tries relentlessly to pull the stake out, attempting thousands of times, but it never has the strength to complete the task. Eventually, after countless futile efforts, it gives up. The elephant grows to full adult size, gaining the strength to easily pull the stake out and free itself. Yet it never tries again. Why? Because it has been chained all its life by the belief that it's too weak to break free. If the elephant could become aware of its full strength, its reality of captivity would shatter in an instant.

Many of us don't realize that when we neglect our true inner strength, we're living out the tale of the elephant in the circus, grown up, but still believing ourselves as limited as we were in the past. Perhaps we once focused our attention on breaking free, but after facing initial defeat, we never developed the awareness to take the right actions to finally succeed. Without the knowledge laid out in this book, many athletes remain unaware of these invisible mental barriers, doomed to the fate of the elephant, struggling again and again, as if still a child, to free themselves. These athletes come to believe that they lack the ability to improve and, as a result, never experience the success of reaching their highest potential.

With the right knowledge, this fate can be avoided. You can realize your strength and effortlessly rip the proverbial stake out of the ground. You can break through barriers and free yourself from blockages. With attention, awareness, and action, you can cultivate the mindset necessary to take your performance to the next level.

SECTION TWO
RESONATING

CHAPTER 4
REALIZATION

"Your own Self-Realization is
the greatest service you can render the world."
— *Ramana Maharshi*

You made it to Section Two of the book. How does it feel? You've completed the Aiming phase, which focused on attention, awareness, and action. The Aiming phase was intended to wake you up. I strongly emphasize the word you. This phase is about understanding the power of attention. It starts with recognizing that this power exists, then becoming aware of its impact in relation to your personal strengths. Finally, attention and awareness join forces, setting you up to take the right actions and advance on the path to triumph.

Section Two is all about Resonating. This section delves into a deep connection with, and understanding of, the self, you. When you think of the word "resonate" or "resonance," think of harmony. It's about being in touch with your most authentic self. This section of the book is my personal favorite, as it guides you to explore the deepest part of yourself. When you can relate to and resonate with that higher inner self, anything becomes possible.

Of course, training is essential, but harmony is about getting in tune with the core self. This isn't something anyone else can describe, determine, or create for you. You already have it within you, and in this section, we'll work to unearth it. Are you ready? Know that this process requires mental fortitude, perseverance, and total honesty with yourself to get the most out of it. Think of it as the prerequisite and rite of passage needed to enter the final phase of the ART system: Tuning.

Now that you understand the journey ahead, let's begin this second phase.

The first "R" in the Resonating phase stands for Realization. In the Aiming phase, we became aware of our potential. Now we take it a step further by realizing its true power. It's the difference between almost having it and truly having it. There's a big difference between awareness and access. Realization of your power means the ability to fully access it. The greatest martial artists and athletes have this ability. They can tap into this well of potential.

To possess this power without using it would be like having an axe to chop wood but only using your hands. Sound like a crazy analogy? It's actually an accurate metaphor for what it's like to know your power yet never put it to full use. So how do we actualize and use this power? What steps can we take to properly cultivate it and bring it into reality?

MISSION STATEMENT

The first step to realizing your power is knowing who you are. This is the starting block, the "core essence" of self-enhancement, as I see it. From this foundation come your values and personal philosophy, which together form your mission statement. Companies use mission statements as a core identifier and guiding light, not only to reach customers on the front lines, but also to mobilize the moving parts of the organization, employees and teams within. If organizations, entities made up of individuals, use this, why shouldn't we apply the same concept to ourselves as individuals, each of us made up of our own parts: physical, mental, emotional, and spiritual?

Whether we're aware of it or not, each of us has a uniquely significant story and personal philosophy. This philosophy is constructed from our values, which come together to form beliefs, and those beliefs shape our belief systems. Think of these belief systems as "programs." They make up the software to your hardware, strongly influencing and dictating your thoughts, emotions, behaviors, and actions. Your mission statement is a signature and calling card of that software. Below, I've provided a series of guiding questions to help you discover and establish it.

These questions all revolve around a singular theme: what is it that you are all about in this life? You might be thinking, "Come on, that's such a loaded question. What does this even have to do with my sport performance?" Didn't I tell you this section would be challenging and would require mental fortitude? Putting that aside, if you had to break down who you are into a few short sentences, what would that look like? Here are some guiding questions to help you craft your mission statement:

- What do you value in life, and why?
- What people or things do you love and care for?
- What are you good or skilled at?
- What traits or characteristics best describe you?
- What would you like your defining traits or characteristics to be?

Reflecting on these questions will help bring clarity to who you are and what you're all about. Now, I must warn you: at this point, an inner voice may start to speak up. This inner voice is the critical self, the judgmental part of you that tries to protect you from accessing the deepest, truest parts of yourself. This part of you wants to stay in the comfort and security of the familiar. It wants to avoid pain at all costs. It fears change. This voice also has a habit of downplaying and nullifying your positive accomplishments, keeping you stagnant and held back.

So be cautious of this inner voice whispering to you from within. When answering the guiding questions above, block out that voice and stay present and nonjudgmental. Have fun with this exercise. Shut off the critical mind and play. This is about enhancing your life, and it's all you have right now, so make it count. Show yourself some love. Give yourself permission to feel what you feel without judgment, and set aside any expectations or limitations about your feelings.

As ironic as it may sound, in the search for your true, authentic self, you must get out of your own way. Doing these exercises and answering these questions are steps toward strengthening and awakening the inner you, making you unstoppable in the outer world.

MY PERSONAL PHILOSOPHY

Earlier, I spoke about a time in competition when I endured a brutal injury yet still came out victorious. What I didn't share then was how I was able to pull that off. As you can guess, it had more to do with personal philosophy than physical prowess. My mission statement, built on core values, beliefs, and mental programs, has long been an integral part of my mental constitution. It's a fundamental set of personal truths that supports my story. That story became an invaluable and reliable source of the strength, determination, and will I needed to win that fight. Now, I want to share those truths with you.

First and foremost, both then and now, I believe there is nothing I cannot accomplish if I truly desire it. The affirmation that best anchors this belief for me is:

"I am truly unstoppable."

Below is a list of other guiding beliefs that programmed me to triumph in the face of overwhelming odds that day:

- I never quit.
- I am a leader.
- I am a role model to others.
- I am a source of strength and inspiration for others.
- I am the one people are counting on. I must never let them down.

There was a lot about me that made me. I'll say that again: there was a lot about me that made me. Looking back on everything that shaped me, the pride I held in my community, the rigorous training I endured, and the unwavering belief my teammates, friends, and family had in me, there was simply no way I was going to fold and quit. I would do whatever it took to ensure I was victorious that day.

At this point, you might be thinking, "Wow, you actually had the time to think all of those things?" The short answer is no. All of this was subconsciously embedded. I wasn't consciously thinking about it, but my inner warrior wouldn't let me quit. All it kept repeating was:

"You've got to find a way to win. You have to do this... you've trained so hard for this moment. You are a warrior!"

And I firmly believe that I am. That belief sits at the core of my personal philosophy. At my core, I am a martial artist. That's exactly why I envisioned creating and sharing the contents of this book with you.

I understand you, the fighter, because I am you. I've lived and experienced the challenges that come with being a competing martial artist. I know the thoughts and inner voices you must navigate and overcome. Because of that, I feel a deep responsibility to pass on the training, teachings, and insights I've gained throughout my journey to you, the reader holding this book right now.

I AM STATEMENTS

The most powerful statement you could ever utter is:

"I AM."

Whatever follows those two words influences and shapes your reality. A few paragraphs ago, I shared the I AM statements ingrained in my subconscious mind, beliefs that kept me from quitting and pushed me to find a way to win. Now it's your turn. What are some I AM statements you can create to help you overcome your personal obstacles and lead you to victory?

Reflect on your values. Think about who you are. Consider the things that hold meaning for you. What do you truly wish for? Most importantly, what empowering beliefs and mental programs do you need in order to achieve and experience the highest version of yourself? Your mission statement holds these values and I AM statements together, forming an internal force that combats external mental oppressors standing in your way. Can you start to see why I titled this book The ART of the Fight?

Trust me when I say there is no greater feeling than being fully in alignment with yourself, rooted in your true power. When you reach that state, nothing can stop you. Obstacles become nothing more than minor bumps and potholes on the road to martial arts mastery.

But reaching this state of being requires effort. It starts with exploring your own truths and building out your I AM statements, your subconscious script. Please take the time to do this before moving on to the next chapter.

Establish a basic mission statement that reflects the values and guiding beliefs you want to live by. This practice will serve you well as we continue forward into the Resonating section of this book.

CHAPTER 5
REVELATION

"Many times revelation doesn't come until
we're moving and pressing forward"
— David A. Bednar

So you have personal power. Now what? In the last chapter, we spoke of realizing this power first through discovering its existence. Hopefully by now, as you are reading this chapter, you have a firm idea of what your values are, what you stand for, and what your mission statement dictates. This serves as your operating system, your compass and North Star. You now know who you are, and that is one of the most powerful insights in the universe. It is said that when you know who you are, you will never again need to be someone or something else.

You have realized your power. But knowing is only half the battle. The best part about personal power, after its realization, is properly utilizing it. This is Revelation.

POWER PROJECTED

This chapter is all about that. At first glance, revelation and realization appear the same. Like the Aiming stage, where attention and awareness are similar, so are the first two phases in this Resonating stage. Consider revelation and realization two sides of the same coin. While they differ, they are also closely linked. Think of realization as the Yin to revelation's Yang.

Realization is that inner understanding, or "inner-standing," of personal power. Revelation involves radiating that power out into the external world. It is walking the walk and talking the talk in the Resonating stage. We are now putting that mission statement and the strengths of who you are into practice. Through daily, repeated behaviors and actions, your personal philosophy is projected outward into your environment and the world.

To drive the point home, revelation is the unveiling of your realization. It is the projection of your power. It is how you show up and handle yourself in your environment day to day. It pulls back the curtain on what resides within you, revealing it to the outside world you interact with. My own personal philosophy showed itself during that fight, despite the severe shoulder injury. The personal power existed all along, yet it was not on display for everyone to experience, not until its revelation.

BY FLOW NOT FORCE

Have you ever caught yourself, or someone else, trying way too hard at something? Perhaps it's during exercise or sport, in social interaction, or in any number of other daily situations. A simple example is driving a car too fast. We've all seen it in some form, that forceful manner of performance, and we've likely done it ourselves. If we're totally honest, we've all been guilty of it at one point or another.

When realizing one's power or ability, especially if it's noticeably great, the first temptation is to openly express it and show it off. Let's return to the analogy of fast driving. Imagine someone newly acquiring a powerful car with lots of horsepower. In most cases, the first desire is to take that car out for a spin, revealing to the world how fast it is.

In the journey of bringing our personal power to the forefront, and ultimately to triumph, we must fully understand how to exercise and ground that power so we can harness it safely, sincerely, and organically. This is what I call flowing rather than forcing. Do by flow, not by force.

For many athletes, realizing their power pushes them to go all in with it. This is where I advise caution. True mastery of one's power does not mean hitting the gas pedal, rapidly climbing from 0 to 100, and burning out. It means being able to combine the science and the art. It means knowing when to turn it up and when to dial it down by understanding rhythm, timing, and pacing. It's channeling the attention discussed in the very first section of this book so you can prevent yourself from overextending and operating under a false sense of confidence, which inevitably crashes.

Ultimate power is power under control. It is the formidable Samurai warrior keeping his sword in the sheath, knowing how and when to wield it with deadly purpose. This manner of performance and being should be your goal. Revelation should come from a state of harmonious flow rather than one of reckless force.

In the final section of the book, we will cover specific techniques and training you can use to put yourself in flow and help you reach that ultimate triumph. For now, heed this cautionary advice: just because you have power does not mean you will apply it properly unless you are aware and paying attention. Stay in the moment, and let power come to you and flow through you. True power is rooted in the knowingness of oneself, and the sovereignty that comes with it. It is living without compromise and without the need for overcompensation.

All that you have is within you. It always has been and always will be. As we begin to realize and reveal this, we move onward to the last section of the Resonating stage: Rise.

CHAPTER 6
RISE

"Still, like air, I rise."
— Maya Angelou

We have arrived at our final stop in the Resonating stage, and that is Rise. Webster's Dictionary defines the word rise as "to move upward." Another definition is "to wake up from sleep, arising from bed." Similar to Maya Angelou's quote, this book is about constant upward movement and progression. The first part of the book was about Aiming, which provided us with direction, grounding, and "earthly" foundations. Now we are set to spread our wings and take to the air.

THE CALL AND CRY

The first part of this stage, Realization, discussed connecting to your internal driving force. Next came Revelation: displaying that force, that personal power, which you've turned your attention toward. Now comes Rise, the awakening of your ideal self.

As you can see, each level builds upon the previous one, giving you a conceptual understanding of the internal work necessary to transform and triumph. Rise is the unification of the work you did in both the Realization and Revelation chapters. You cannot rise like air without first understanding the power in your possession, and then being able to exercise that power properly in service of your goals.

It becomes necessary to awaken that ideal version of you. This is a definitive call to action and a cry to be fully you.

WAKE UP

For many, this is difficult because most are still "asleep at the wheel." Their attention is scattered and, on top of that, there is no intention behind it. The result is an endless, habitual cycle of disconnection between who you are currently and who you wish, and were meant, to be.

This disconnect leads to severe shortcomings in life experience when compared to what you would, could, and should have. This book provides the knowledge to ensure that the desired life experience is, rather than would, could, or should be.

So what is rising? It is the real you, not just an aspect, but all of you, completely unified. If you've made it this far into the book and are applying what you have learned, it means the real you is beginning to awaken and arise.

If you are doing the work in this book, then your best and brightest version of yourself will shine, as sure as the sun rises every morning. It's the rise that you, and those around you, need. It's the rise that allows your efforts to inspire others, granting them equal permission to rise as well.

EXITING RESONATING

Before we enter the final stage of the ART system, "T" for Tuning, here are a few parting thoughts, posed as questions, that I'd like to leave you with:

Do you know who you are?

Do you understand why you are?

Do you accept and allow yourself to be all that you are?

I leave you with these thoughts because without them, you cannot apply yourself properly in the next phase. This upcoming stage presents the actual workout. It is where you will break that mental sweat, as you put down the book, pick up the pen, and begin burning some mental calories.

We are beginning the proverbial fight camp. Up to this point, we were in off-season training. Now this is the moment preceding the moment of triumph.

This is what you have been waiting for and inching toward. It is the reason you picked up this book. Now the questions finally cease, and the answers that will land you exactly where you want to be begin to flow.

With that said, see you in the Tuning phase.

SECTION THREE
TUNING

CHAPTER 7
TECHNIQUE

*"Art is technique: a means by which to materialize
the invisible realm of the mind."*
— *Hiroshi Sugimoto*

las, we arrive at the final section of this book: Tuning. The previous two stages, Aiming and Resonating, have prepared us for this one. In Stage One, we gather attention, channel awareness, and take action toward the performance problems and issues we wish to solve. In Stage Two, we come to a clear realization of who we are, display that personal power through revelation, and finally rise to the level of the ideal person we want and need to be. This is what is required in order to experience the highest, most potentiated version of yourself and your reality.

This section covers the following three parts: Technique, Training, and Triumph.

Each of these segments will guide you in reaching and tapping into your unstoppable self, and show you how to consistently stay in that state of performance and living. Think of it like playing Super Mario. Remember that game? Do you recall the moments when Mario is unstoppable and can literally mow through his enemies? This only happens when he attains star power. When he has it, we hear that epic musical jingle accompanying a state of invincibility as he runs straight through his foes. I share this analogy to give you an idea of what applying the practical strategies in this section can feel like when done successfully. Through this stage, you are learning specific, applicable methods for developing that "star-like" capability to master the external forces, your opponents in sport and in life, coming at you.

Tuning is about dialing into that frequency, the state of mental vibration needed to act as your ideal self. The ability to enter this state freely allows you to maximize your achievements, bringing about triumph in all manner of endeavors. This section breaks down the process of learning and practicing to attain such a state. You will discover techniques that martial artists, such as yourself, can use to bring attention, awareness, and action to the forefront.

These techniques will serve as practices you can engage in on a daily basis. With consistent, earnest work, you are on the road to self-mastery. Upon learning the techniques, you can then work to apply them through the Training section. This is where we get into details and specifics, such as sample plans and routines, which you can plug and play according to your needs, to help you start seeing improvements in your sport performance.

The ultimate resulting triumph is the marriage of information and application. It is joining together all that you are, as a martial artist and human being, to help you enter that winning state of flow. When you put together all the elements learned within this book, you will more easily be able to pull and attract what you desire regarding performance, instead of straining in endless pursuit of it. Let's begin, shall we?

MENTAL TRAINING TECHNIQUES

You've likely heard of mindfulness, a mental meta-skill that has been receiving a growing amount of attention and study over the last decade or so. Headspace, a popular app that helps people develop mindfulness, defines it as "the quality of being present and fully engaged with whatever you're doing at the moment." This also means being free of judgment and distraction as you pay attention.

Mindfulness often goes hand in hand with meditation. Trust me when I say this is an important skill to tap into and harness as a martial artist. It's where the attention and awareness from Section One really come into play. This is why the book has been laid out in the sequence provided: to culminate in helping you present your very best self in the moments you need it most, translating mental skills into brilliant physical execution.

Not too long ago, I wrote a detailed article that breaks down meditation and how relevant it is for us athletes. I've included the article below so you can get an in-depth understanding of the practice. I have one request, however, before sharing it with you: do not skip over it. There will be a temptation to skim, but doing so would be a mistake. Up to this point, if you have been following the format of this book to the letter, then you are well aware of how each part is relevant and useful to grasping the whole. The same applies to this article, so let's get to it.

MEDITATION

The purpose of this article is to provide a primer on meditation and simplify, or demystify, the practice. The hope and intention in doing so is to lower its "barrier of entry" and allow more of you to begin implementing it as a tool for personal enhancement.

First, what is meditation?

"Meditation refers to a family of techniques
which have in common a conscious
attempt to focus attention in a non-
analytical way and an attempt not to dwell
on discursive, ruminating thought."
— Shapiro, 1982

The above is a formal definition often referenced in psychology literature.

My own interpretation defines meditation as the practice of cultivating and developing one's attentive abilities by bringing the person into awareness of their inner world (physical body and mental processes) and outer world (environment and surroundings).

One thing not touched on in my definition, which the formal definition highlights, is the non-analytical way of focusing one's attention. Right after that is the mention of avoiding dwelling on thoughts.

This is crucial because a common misconception is that one has to be perfectly clear and empty of thoughts in order for meditation to be successful. Of course, this is nearly impossible to attain when first starting the practice. As a result, people get discouraged and drift away from it when they are unable to meet this expectation.

The key takeaway from the above paragraphs is that we can simplify meditation to the practice of developing mind-body awareness in the present moment. We do this by using techniques, which we will discuss shortly, to focus our attention in a nonjudgmental, non-analytical way.

Alright, so how do we do this? There are many ways, but it helps to break it down into two categories: static and dynamic.

Think of static meditation as the traditional picture we have: an individual sitting in some kind of pose, with eyes closed, doing breath work to enter a trance-like state. I would categorize any seated, lying, or standing (but still) meditation under this category.

Dynamic meditation has many examples. This is essentially performing some kind of movement while continuing present-centered awareness and maintaining focus on mind-body in relation to the task and the environment it is being carried out in. Walking, light jogging, biking, painting, playing music, doing yoga, stretching, and mobility work can all fall under this category.

An important thing to note here is that once the activity becomes too intense, it would no longer fall under meditative practice. A prerequisite for meditation is that it keeps us in a parasympathetic-dominant state. This is the "rest and digest" state of the autonomic nervous system. Any practice that begins to elevate the heart rate and take us into a sympathetic state would be classified as exercise at that point.

Having said that, this does not mean that one cannot exercise and still meditate, in the sense of focusing one's attention in a non-analytical way.

So, getting back to meditation, we can either practice it statically or dynamically. The next important piece in building a solid practice is to use the breath as the focal point. There are many excellent breathing techniques, some to induce relaxation and others to induce excitation. For the purpose of meditation, we want to focus on relaxation breathing.

The essence of this is learning to breathe diaphragmatically. The cue I always give is "deep belly breaths." You can place one hand over the navel and the other over the chest to confirm that you are taking diaphragmatic breaths. If the top hand moves or rises first, then you know the breathing is shallow. The first two-thirds of the breath should fill the lower diaphragm, and then the final third fills the upper half.

Practice this "complete breathing" technique, paying attention to the air as it enters through the nostrils, fills the diaphragm, and then is released through the mouth or through the nose again. Set a timer for 3 to 5 minutes and let the breathing guide you. Pay no mind (pun intended) to the thoughts and "mental chatter" going on. Over time, you will learn to naturally quiet your mind and be present in your environment. It all begins with the breath.

At the very minimum, you will feel more relaxed and calm at the end of your 3 to 5 minutes of complete breathing. This, my friends, is meditation. It helps you de-stress and center before starting your day, or it can act as a quick mental and physical break between long bouts of work. You can even use this specific static meditation before bed to wind down.

The point is this: meditation can be very simple to practice, yet profoundly effective in changing the course of your day by allowing you to stay more relaxed and present. The long-term effects of practicing for merely 5 minutes a day are vast. Give it a shot today.

You should now have a much better understanding of meditation after reading the article above. Hopefully you can start to see its immense value, and how it can contribute to helping you develop into a higher-performing version of yourself. As mentioned, at the very least, you are able to better relax and still yourself. Meditation can help bring us into a desired state of balance and calmness, allowing a syncing up of our inner and outer worlds. It is in this state that all the magic happens.

With just a few minutes of work, you can be on your way to approaching the world with a more positive outlook while staying in the present moment, free of past or future troubles.

And for those of you healthy skeptics who may rightfully doubt the efficacy of this technique, let me share an experience with one of my mental performance coaching athletes. He was a high-level soccer player whom I implemented meditation with to help him get more out of practice sessions. He would simply do deep breathing for about 5 minutes, as described in the article. Additionally, he practiced imagery and visualization, which we'll discuss next, but it all started with getting him to breathe properly and mindfully. We primarily worked on developing and practicing the complete breath, that diaphragmatic breathing discussed earlier.

What were the results? He felt more prepared going into practice, and he reported feeling relaxed but alert. Does that last part ring any bells? This is what applying this technique can do for you. You can program yourself to remain calm in moments that require high-level problem solving, the kind we've talked about. That is invaluable for the fighter.

There is another technique I would like to share with you. It aligns nicely with meditation, but differs enough that it warrants its own section.

IMAGERY / VISUALIZATION

Elite athletes are notorious for visualization. Have you seen images of athletes, such as Michael Phelps, prior to competition? What do they look like? What are they doing? Some have headphones on, others don't, but if you pay attention, you will notice these athletes using imagery.

The question is why. Why are they doing this, and what are the performance benefits of using these techniques? How does it lead someone to experience that moment of victory, that triumph?

Like meditation, visualization is powerful. Before diving further into it, it's important that we understand one thing. Visualization is simply a tool with a single purpose: bringing a desired state into your present moment. It is meant to help us properly direct our energy, our attention, and become aware of the feelings that come along with those images so we can create reference points. Once those reference points are established, they are no longer needed. You begin living it. The connection has been made, and access has been granted.

There's a quote in Zen Buddhism that goes, "Rivers become rivers, mountains become mountains again." Essentially, it means that once you reach a state of mastery and put this into practice, it becomes natural to you, as much a part of you as your hands and legs. You can let it all go, relinquish control, and allow yourself to just be. You are true to your own nature. This is the ultimate state to pursue. This is the moment of triumph.

Look at animals in nature. What do you think goes through their minds? Predators don't have to read books on hunting effectively. Tigers don't need to read books on running faster. Nor do eagles need to listen to podcasts on flying with confidence. See what I'm getting at here? They are just being what they are. They are being natural.

That is what we are aiming for, and that is ultimately what the martial arts are: a study and representation of nature expressed through human movement. I would extend this by saying that engaging in any kind of art form is a way to get in touch with nature. This is why so many people can get lost and enrapt in artistic pursuits, whether it's martial arts, dancing, painting, playing music, you name it. That is what the flow state is: the human being returning to its natural state.

I know that was a preamble for visualization, but I hope it paints an adequate picture of its enormous potential for life and performance enhancement. As mentioned earlier, our thoughts become things, and everything starts on a mental level. Everything begins on the mental plane. You have to imagine and, most importantly, feel it before it becomes a physical reality. Anything that has ever been created, buildings, tools, technologies, systems of any kind, began as a thought first. Think (pun intended) about that. We are living in a world of constant creation, expansion, and manifestation, all originating from mind.

MORE THAN PICTURES

This all speaks to the power of visualization and imagination, something all human beings have access to as an inherent gift. No other animal on Earth, that we know of, is capable of such an ability. The problem is that we humans have lost sight of it. Instead of harnessing this power, most of us have let ourselves become controlled by it. We visualize self-defeating scenarios, anxiety-inducing situations, and failed outcomes. When we let our imagination run wild and unchecked, we defeat ourselves before any opponent in life ever could. We need to become aware again. We need to reclaim our power.

Visualization is one key practice that can be used to start shaping one's reality. The power of visualization is not only in forming an image, but also in attaching a feeling to it. It's not until we charge our images with positive emotion that we have something we can begin to physically manifest.

Once we have an image that is highly charged with powerful emotion, it starts to become real, and action toward its physical actualization begins. Conor McGregor, and many other champions for that matter, is a strong example of this. Multiple interviews have captured him speaking about the power of visualization. ESPN featured a short video segment on how McGregor manifested his professional career success. In the video, he said things like, "I manifested my double championship, winning my two belts. I saw this a long time ago, holding two belts in the air." I believe it was this line of thinking that helped him achieve what few ever have in the sport of mixed martial arts. Winning in multiple weight classes and attaining such titles required more than hard work and physical prowess. It required him seeing what was possible as his reality and believing in it so intensely that it became fact.

Here is a statement from McGregor on visualization:

"If you have a clear picture in your head that something is going to happen and a clear belief that it will happen no matter what, then nothing can stop it. It is destined to happen. It is perfect."

Powerful stuff.

VISUALIZATION FOR ALL

All of us have this ability, this gift. Becoming aware of it and learning to harness its power can be of tremendous benefit. We can use visualization, the art of imagery, to architect our day-to-day reality. By visualizing how we would like things to play out, and then feeling its effects in real time, we can begin to map out the days, weeks, months, and even years ahead.

For those who have never practiced visualization before, it begins with a script. This is what I've used with my athletes. Think of the script as training wheels. Once you are able to create your intended images with vivid detail and feeling, you'll find that the process becomes second nature. Many people, at first, may struggle to create those moving mental pictures, which is why a script is a useful starting aid.

VISUALIZATION FRAMEWORK

The framework for visualization begins with a set of bullet points. These bullet points should form the scene of what you wish to achieve, your desired outcome in performance. After you create those bullet points, turn them into full sentences. Next, shape those sentences into a story by giving it structure: a beginning, middle, and end.

When crafting your story, be sure to add meaningful words that evoke emotion and target the senses. The more of your five senses you include, the more effective the imagery. In your visualized scene, what do you feel tactilely? What sounds do you hear? Are there any smells or tastes? The greater the detail, the more powerful this practice will be.

Once you have this part down, record yourself reading the story out loud, narrating in the first person. It's important to keep your story positive and empowering. This is about bringing out your ideal self, so let that voice guide you. It also reinforces proper self-talk, affirming to yourself that you matter and that what you think takes priority and becomes reality. This practice helps you hone the unstoppable quality and personal power discussed in the Realization phase of this book.

Remember, it's not about having the perfect story, so don't sweat the tiny details. Make sure the words carry meaning for you, and that they make you feel that successful, desired performance in real time.

Like the other techniques, this serves as a tool to help you process the look and feel of victory and ultimate triumph. Once you put this into practice and really get the hang of it, you will no longer need a premeditated script as a guide. You'll become your own natural guide in visualization.

In the next chapter, where we introduce the actual Training phase, you will find an example of a visualization script to reference when designing yours. It can and should be modified to fit your specific situation, given that each athlete's needs differ with varying levels of awareness.

CHAPTER 8
TRAINING

"I hated every minute of training, but I said, Don't quit.
Suffer now and live the rest of your life as a champion.
— *Muhammad Ali*

n the last chapter, you learned key techniques to help you tune into your ideal self. Now, in this chapter, there will be less theory and more application. It's time to put everything we've been talking about into action. I learned long ago that information changes nothing in your life until you apply it. It's the application of information that leads to transformation. We are turning knowledge into self-knowledge, as Bruce Lee would put it. As you complete this book and apply what you've learned, you are developing the kind of self-knowledge that leads to the triumph we've been alluding to, the triumph of transformation.

This section provides sample routines you can begin implementing into your daily regimen to start seeing results in your mental performance, which, in turn, positively influences your physical performance. Like any training, results do not come overnight. Think about the difference between when you first learned to throw a punch or kick and where you are now. The same goes for the grappler who learned to become comfortable in basic ground positions. As martial artists, we know this difference well, and we understand how much consistent time and effort it takes to span the gap between learning and mastery.

The routines provided are only as good as the effort you put in. The more you practice, the more they will become yours, turning into true self-knowledge. Initially, these exercises may feel foreign, and that's perfectly normal. Like learning to ride a bicycle, you will adjust, adapt, and grow familiar with them. Before you know it, these practices will merge with habit, becoming a regular part of your positive mental conditioning.

Let's dive into the routines below. After each one, I'll provide notes to highlight where your attention should be and what you can expect from each exercise.

RELAXATION BREATHWORK

Attaining a calm mind-body state is essential to getting the most out of any mental skill. When we are relaxed, we are in a parasympathetic state, the "rest and digest" state of the nervous system, as opposed to the "fight or flight" state, which is most ideal for competition. The ability to switch between these two states is an invaluable skill in itself, demonstrating control over one's physiological state, which is connected to the mind and emotions. To control one is to influence the rest.

So how do we work toward achieving this degree of control and personal mastery? The answer lies in the breath. You may have heard of Wim Hof. If you want to see the power of breath work, look at the feats he accomplishes through mastery of breathing.

We won't be diving into the Wim Hof Method, but rather a simpler and more foundational step: practicing deep diaphragmatic breathing, also known as the Complete Breath.

Breathe slowly and deeply in through the nose, filling the belly area (just beneath the navel) with air first. Go at an easy pace. Never force the breath or overdo the inhalation. As you feel the lower torso filling, allow the breath to fill the lower chest, then the upper chest. Imagine the air filling you like a balloon, bringing you into tall posture at full inhalation.

You may either hold the breath for 1 to 3 seconds, or proceed right away to exhale through the nose or mouth. Let the air leave your body slowly and naturally, moving from the upper to lower torso, the opposite of how it entered.

Repeat this complete breath for 3 to 5 minutes and you will find yourself in a more relaxed state than when you started.

Frequency
1 to 2 times per day
Prior to bedtime
Prior to training
Optional: anytime you want a relaxed, calm state

Duration
3 to 5 minutes

Pro tip
Do not worry about racing thoughts. Bring your focus back to your breath as best you can.

MINDFULNESS

Mindfulness is the art of living in, and paying attention to, the present moment in a nonjudgmental manner.

While that definition is accurate, it only scratches the surface of its value. Mindfulness is a tool, a practice, and ultimately an art for understanding yourself. It is a pathway to discovering your own personal power and potential, not only as a martial artist, but as a human being.

Remember: energy flows where attention goes. Think of attention as the muscle of mindfulness. By working and flexing it, you become more adept at directing your focus where it needs to be, ideally, in the present moment. When you fully apply this to your physical training, especially in sparring or fighting, your performance becomes more powerful.

This exercise is simple but highly effective for developing greater mind-body awareness. The key is to work that mindfulness muscle by paying attention and being present to yourself and your environment.

There are four levels to this practice:

1. Low stimuli: sitting or lying down, eyes open or closed, in isolation in a quiet, controlled environment.
   Example: sitting in a chair in your room or office with calming sounds or total silence.

2. Medium stimuli: sitting or walking, eyes open, in a minimally populated, fairly quiet environment.

Example: walking in your neighborhood or park by yourself. The area should be quiet or have minimal noise.

3. High stimuli: walking or driving in a populated, noisy, busy environment while engaging with your surroundings.
Example: being at the grocery store among others. Having a conversation with someone.

4. Game stimuli: heavy movement, such as training or practicing your sport or discipline, with an elevated heart rate.
Example: sparring, rolling, or any skills training.

Each level presents a greater challenge to your ability to stay attentive and mindful in the present. This means paying attention to your internal world (physiology, sensations, thoughts, feelings), as well as your external world (environment, sounds, temperature, smells).

Start at the first level and work your way up, incrementally building your mindfulness ability.

Frequency
1 to 2 times per day
Whenever appropriate

Duration
5 minutes

Pro tip

Start at the low level first, and only move up when you feel able to stay present without being distracted or mentally wandering.

VISUALIZATION / IMAGERY

Imagery, or visualization, is one of the cornerstones of mental conditioning. Through the power of imagination, we can "hack" reality and help the brain and body believe in what is being visualized. The more vivid the details, the more likely you are to replicate the desired performance in real life.

Think of the movie The Matrix, and how the characters download programs for fighting, weapons, or even flying a helicopter. The idea is that, to the brain, there is little difference between what we imagine and what we live out in the real world.

The more you grasp the power of visualization for enhancing performance, building confidence, and reducing fear, the more you'll realize its importance as a supplement to physical training. Imagery is an accelerator for your performance.

All tools need sharpening for optimal use, and the same goes for imagery. Some will find visualization effortless, while others will need practice. Regardless, it's an innate talent we all possess. Think back to childhood. You likely used your imagination constantly, whether you remember it or not. This is a natural gift, and reawakening it is key.

The best way I've found to help clients build this skill is by using an imagery script, as discussed earlier. Bring in as much vivid sensory detail as possible. Try to include as many of the five senses as you can. There's no single right way. Use what feels strongest for you and creates a moving image with powerful emotion, which is the most important part.

As Bruce Lee said: "Don't think. Feel. We need emotional content."

Below is a sample visualization script. As you get comfortable, you'll move beyond words, running the scenario in your mind as if you were watching a movie. Ultimately, it's the feeling that charges the scene and brings it to life, even more than the images themselves.

Sample visualization script

"I arrive at my gym, feeling strong, healthy, and excited to train. I am calm, yet ready to get active. I greet my friends and fellow training partners, having some light conversation as I set my gear down and begin doing dynamic stretching. I am grateful to be here and cannot wait to begin the session. Our warmup is perfect and serves to get my body loose and my mind ready for drilling techniques.

We begin working basic striking combinations. My timing feels sharp. Each time I repeat the combination, I feel myself dialing in further and further. The sound of my gloves hitting the pads is music to my ears. I am completely in the present moment and tuned into my body.

Next, we move into sparring. I begin my first round with a training partner. Everything is flowing nicely. I am relaxed yet alert, managing my energy well. My breathing is steady and rhythmic. I am light and mobile on my feet. My reflexes feel sharp as I anticipate every punch thrown by my sparring partner. I counter well, landing punches and turning defense into offense. I feel confident in my ability, and I am having fun being in the moment and enjoying the competitive pressure my partner is giving me.

The round ends. We touch gloves, and I move to a new sparring partner. I adjust to my new opponent's movements and tendencies. I am able to read and pick up patterns effortlessly. It feels like time is slowing down, and I am in the Matrix. It is truly amazing. I love fighting, and I love training."

Note: the above script is intentionally positive in its performance details. However, it's perfectly fine, and even encouraged, to include challenging moments, such as your opponent landing some shots that you later adjust to. This makes the imagery more realistic. If your script is too perfect too soon, it may not be as readily accepted by the brain as reality.

Frequency
1 to 2 times per day
In the morning
Prior to your training session

Duration
5 to 10 minutes

Pro tip
Practice diaphragmatic breathing as you visualize.

THINKING HEART MEDITATION

The Thinking Heart Meditation (THM) is a meta-technique that combines relaxation, mindfulness, and imagery, or visualization. This blend is designed to help you attain a relaxed mind-body state while improving your mental rehearsal ability. The intent is to enhance self-confidence in performance accomplishment through vivid imagery, immersing you in your desired outcome. By acting as if, you replicate this performance and ingrain it into both conscious and subconscious awareness.

Sit comfortably with your back supported and your feet flat on the ground. Close your eyes and let yourself settle into the chair.

Take three slow, deep, complete breaths. With each exhale, relax further as you release tension.

Place your awareness at your feet, noticing any tension and softening that body part. Gradually work your way up, segment by segment, toward your head.

Begin to imagine your desired scene or state. Place yourself in that environment. What do you see? Hear? Smell? Taste? Feel? What are you doing? How are you performing? What does it feel like to succeed?

Imagine the scene playing like a film in your mind. Now, mentally bring that moving image down from your head into your chest. You are now feeling the scene through your heart. Immerse yourself in the positive emotions, acting completely as if you have achieved the desired outcome.

As you continue breathing naturally, allow yourself to sit with these positive feelings as the scene plays out. When you're ready, bring your attention back to your body and open your eyes.

Frequency
3 to 5 times per week

Duration

Minimum: 10 minutes

3 to 5 minutes relaxation

1 to 2 minutes mindfulness

2 to 3 minutes imagery

Pro tip

If the scene you visualize energizes you, such as fighting or sparring, avoid doing this right before bed, as it may make it harder to wind down.

CHAPTER 9
TRIUMPH

"At the best knows in the end the
triumph of high achievement."
— *Theodore Roosevelt*

Congratulations.

Well, not just yet. But I do want to commend you for making it to the final chapter of this book.

Mental conditioning is essential for all athletes, especially combat athletes, because so much is on the line given the nature of the sport itself. You've done the work and followed the processes laid out in these pages, all to reach this final destination: Triumph.

In the previous two chapters of this Tuning section, you gained knowledge of powerful techniques and received specific routines to help you apply that knowledge, turning it into self-knowledge. This is Triumph: the fusion of knowledge and application coming together to shape your ideal self. Triumph is both an outcome and a state of being.

No longer is your ideal self some distant dream or illusion. You know more about yourself now than ever before, and with that comes power. The awareness and actualization of who you are, and the force that lies within, places you at a true competitive advantage.

You are now positioned to triumph, not merely because you are strong, but because you have had the courage to press into the deepest recesses of your mind and spirit. The opening quote for this chapter, about courage and triumph, represents who you are now. It takes discipline, persistence, and true courage to do the inner work so that you may reveal your greatness to the world, shining with truth, goodness, and conviction.

Triumph is walking with this newly acquired self-knowledge every day. Remember to use this knowledge wisely and responsibly. In the immortal words of Uncle Ben Parker: "With great power comes great responsibility." As stated before, reckless application would be a misuse of your newfound power, so heed this counsel. Masters understand how much is needed, and when to use it. That is my hope for you.

Also bear in mind that attaining this state does not guarantee you will never again face loss, hardship, or defeat. These are natural parts of life. However, through this evolved and upgraded self, which this book aims to help you attain, you will always have the ability to turn tragedy into triumph. The process you have learned here is not a one-time occurrence. It is a system you can deploy at will whenever you need it. I hope that is something you've truly come to realize.

THE MARATHON CONTINUES

The power you now have access to is ongoing. The processes and practices for cultivating personal power are only as effective as the effort you put into them. This journey is continuous and cyclical, and it should go without saying that you only get back what you put in. Your honest effort throughout this process is what brings about real triumph.

As you fully immerse yourself in the practices laid out in this book, cycling through victories and defeats, you will continue to grow, improve, evolve, and achieve even greater triumphs. Remember, this journey will include many pit stops. You will experience loss. However, if you learn from it, you will never truly experience a pitfall.

There's a saying: "It's not winning or losing; it's winning and learning." This is what people at the top of their game understand. Every experience can be beneficial and useful, providing an opportunity to move forward and upward on your path to becoming, and living as, your absolute best self.

This is what mental conditioning is, and should always be, about.

FINAL WORDS

There is no such thing as absolute loss or defeat. Remember: there are pit stops, and there are pitfalls. Stopping is not falling. Losing is learning. True defeat does not exist without your permission. Short of physical death, there is no defeat, challenge, or obstacle that cannot be overcome. Most of what stops people is mental.

This is not to discount real hardships, disability, poverty, hunger, sickness, abuse, that a smaller percentage of people, unfortunately, must face. I do not minimize or reduce the weight of those realities. But for those reading this book, fortunate enough to pursue and practice something they love, the primary challenges ahead will be mental ones.

Problems are just that: problems. As surely as they arise, so too can solutions, provided you maintain the right level of awareness and a steady rhythm of action. The key is to resonate with the solution, gradually tuning into its frequency, and thereby creating triumph. There is no end. There is always a way.

When you are certain that the way exists, you cannot be stopped.

Your mental conditioning journey with this book is now complete, but in truth, the voyage is just beginning. It is, and always will be, never-ending. "Love the journey," as my coach would always say with enthusiasm. Take what you have learned here and share it with others. Engage with this knowledge, and invite others of like mind to join you on the journey. After all, a road traveled with friends is more meaningful, and may be paved with greater intention, focus, and passion.

You are ready for the next level. I am grateful you have allowed me to guide you this far. May you live and experience your absolute best self, and all that you dream, in the odyssey of life. And when challenges and hardships inevitably appear on your upward path, may you conquer them fearlessly by embracing the ART of the Fight.

ACKNOWLEDGEMENTS

To my parents, Jafar Hassanzadeh and Simin Alamooty, for raising me, supporting me, showing unending kindness, and helping me become the man I am today.

To my martial arts teachers, coaches, and mentors over the years, Stan Kendricks, Todd Santo, Everest Pepper, Ralph King, and Jivoni Paul Jordan, each of whom has influenced me by shaping my training and helping me realize the warrior within.

To all my training partners and brothers and sisters-in-arms, my IMC, ASD, and MU family. You know who you are.

Special thanks to Ryan Lee and Geo Derice for helping me cultivate this book idea and bring it into physical form.

And to all friends and loved ones who have supported me and been there for me throughout my life, in both tragedy and triumph. Our experiences, both good and bad, especially the bad, have the power to teach and mold us into stronger, deeper people, so long as we acknowledge and accept them as life's greatest teachers.

With that, I also give thanks for the struggles and "pain teachers," battles with severe physical and mental illness that could have taken my life on more than one occasion. Fate, and perhaps sheer determination, allowed me to survive, come out stronger, and develop a resolve to empower others, a gift I will always be grateful for.

Those fights in life have given me more strength, will, wisdom, and heart than any bout in the ring ever could.

ABOUT THE AUTHOR

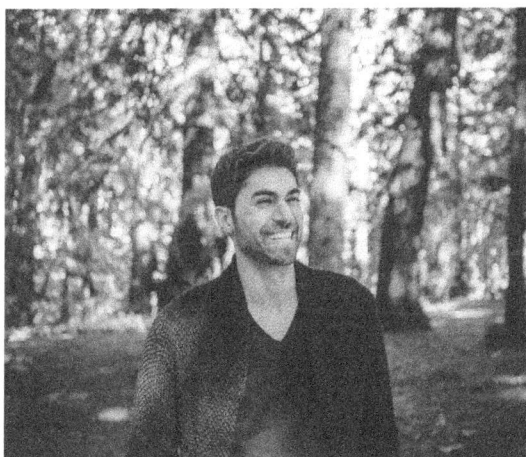

Sepano Hassanzadeh is a performance coach, martial artist, and actor based in the California Bay Area. He is dedicated to inspiring and empowering individuals to realize their true potential by mastering both movement and mindset.

Over the past 15 years, Sepano has worked with hundreds of clients in the health, fitness, and wellness space, and has taught martial arts and self-defense to people of all ages and backgrounds. He is known for blending traditional wisdom with modern performance psychology to help individuals and combat athletes unlock their highest capabilities.

Sepano holds a Master's degree in Sport Psychology (2020), along with numerous certifications in wellness, holistic lifestyle coaching, nutrition, and personal fitness training. He is a Certified Strength and Conditioning Specialist (CSCS) and an advocate for holistic, integrative approaches to health and human performance.

His passion lies at the intersection of physical excellence, mental mastery, and spiritual growth. As the creator of the ART System, a framework for mental conditioning, he guides martial artists and performers to break through mental and physical barriers, develop unshakable confidence, and achieve peak performance both on and off the mat.

Beyond coaching, Sepano is also an actor, storyteller, and lifelong student of the martial arts. His mission is to empower combat athletes and high performers to discover and wield their true power, leaving a positive and lasting legacy in their own lives and communities.

You can connect with Sepano and explore his latest teachings, resources, and programs below.

Contact Info

Website:

COACHSEPANO.COM

Email:

sepanohassanzadeh@gmail.com

Youtube:

https://www.youtube.com/@coachsepano

www.ingramcontent.com/pod-product-compliance
Lightning Source LLC
Chambersburg PA
CBHW031222090426
42740CB00007B/667